STERLING CHILDREN'S BOOKS
New York

An Imprint of Sterling Publishing Co., Inc.
1166 Avenue of the Americas
New York, NY 10036

ISBN 978-1-4549-2380-0

Distributed in Canada by Sterling Publishing Co., Inc.
c/o Canadian Manda Group, 664 Annette Street
Toronto, Ontario M6S 2C8, Canada
Distributed in the United Kingdom by GMC Distribution Services
Castle Place, 166 High Street, Lewes, East Sussex BN7 1XU, England
Distributed in Australia by NewSouth Books
University of New South Wales, Sydney, NSW 2052, Australia

For information about custom editions, special sales, and premium and corporate purchases, please
contact Sterling Special Sales at 800-805-5489 or specialsales@sterlingpublishing.com.

Manufactured in China

Lot #:
2 4 6 8 10 9 7 5 3 1
01/19

sterlingpublishing.com

Cover and endpaper design by Julie Robine and Heather Kelly
Interior design by Julie Robine

Additional photo credits
JumKit/Shutterstock: 7; Sarawut Kundej/Shutterstock: 15

CLOWNFISH
Aren't So FUNNY

**FASCINATING FACTS ABOUT SOME OF THE
OCEAN'S MOST MISUNDERSTOOD CREATURES**

by Matt Weiss

photos by Matt Weiss & Keri Wilks

STERLING CHILDREN'S BOOKS
New York

While sharks, whales, and dolphins get plenty of attention, the real drama of the ocean takes place in the nooks and crannies of coral reefs, sea-grass beds, and the sandy seafloor of tropical oceans. The ocean is made up of ecosystems, communities of living organisms that interact with one another and their environment. Some of these ecosystems, such as coral reefs, consist of as many as 9 million species. That's more people than there are in New York City on a crowded workday! However, if you don't look closely, you might never see many of these amazing animals. And that's a shame, because they have some of the best stories in the entire animal kingdom. Some of the coolest critters are often no bigger than a golf ball and stay hidden from plain sight. From clownfish to emperor shrimp to pygmy seahorses, read on to discover the surprising stories of the ocean's smaller inhabitants.

CLOWNFISH FACTS

- SIZE: 3-6 inches
- HABITAT: Shallow reefs of the Indian and Pacific Oceans
- DIET: Algae and plankton
- FUN FACT: It is one of the few animals that can withstand an anemone sting.

CLOWNFISH

Clownfish aren't so funny! Don't let their name fool you—they are not all fun and games. These fish are relatively common in coral reefs throughout the Pacific Ocean. They have a special relationship with another animal called an anemone that has lots of stinging tentacles. However, because clownfish have special skin that prevents them from getting stung by anemones, they live among the tentacles. When another animal appears to threaten them, clownfish are known to aggressively protect their homes, repeatedly attacking potential intruders much bigger than they are. Divers often report being bitten by clownfish. So while they may look cute, and have a silly name, don't expect them to back down to anybody—even you!

FLYING GURNARD

A fish that flies? Well, the flying gurnard does not fly in the air, but it has fins that make it look as if it is gliding across the ocean. This bottom-dwelling fish spends most of its time hanging out on the seafloor. However, when it gets excited, it can extend its modified pectoral fins, the fins on the sides of the fish, so that they look like wings. That allows the fish to swim quickly around the ocean. And while it's not actually flying, it does confuse potential predators who are often scared off by its large, wing-like fins. When the gurnard isn't "flying" it can use those special pectoral fins to walk around the seafloor, poking around the sand and mud for critters it may be able to eat. There are reports, however, of seeing flying gurnards glide above the water for short periods of time. So, maybe it is a flying fish after all!

EMPEROR SHRIMP

Emperor shrimp aren't really emperors at all. In fact, they are tiny shrimp that barely reach an inch long. What they lack in size, however, they make up for in beauty. Emperor shrimp get their name from their bright colors, but they don't do much ruling. These passive shrimp usually spend their days hitching a ride on the bottom of sea cucumbers or large nudibranchs (which are like snails without shells). They go wherever the sea cucumber goes, happy to have a free ride. The shrimp also gets its food from its host, eating parasites off the sea cucumber's body. Hanging out on the backside of a sea cucumber doesn't seem very royal to me!

SOLAR-POWERED NUDIBRANCH

No, the solar-powered nudibranch is not an energy-conscious nudibranch, but it is still a fascinating critter! Nudibranchs are like snails, but they don't have shells. Many are tiny, but the solar-powered nudibranch can be the size of a football. It's named after the fact that it harvests algae that can *photosynthesize* just like plants. *Photosynthesis* is fancy word that describes algae and plants' ability to turn energy from the sun into food. Solar-powered nudibranchs eat soft coral, which has a little algae inside of it, and are then able to store the algae in their bodies. The algae can then create food to feed both themselves and the nudibranch! This is like carrying a restaurant around with you at all times.

DAMSELFISH

You would imagine that, with a name like damselfish, these fish sit around all day trying to look pretty. But while some of them are quite beautiful, damselfish are actually known for being the ocean's gardeners. Damselfish move their favorite algae near their homes so it can grow nearby. They even remove the other algae in the garden to make room for the one they like to eat, just as gardeners remove weeds! They work so hard on these gardens that, like clownfish, they are relentless about protecting their bounty. This is no damsel in distress!

CUTTLEFISH FACTS

- SIZE: 3 inches
- HABITAT: Indo-Pacific waters off northern Australia, southern New Guinea, the Philippines, Indonesia, and Malaysia.
- DIET: Small shrimp, crabs, and fish
- FUN FACT: Flamboyant cuttlefish are born with their amazing colors.

CUTTLEFISH

Don't try to cuddle a cuttlefish! All cuttlefish are closely related to the octopus and the squid. The one shown here is known as a flamboyant cuttlefish. To those who love them, they are affectionately known as flambos. These guys only reach about three inches long, but they are among the most beautiful animals in the ocean. Flambos can display stunning patterns, colors, and textures, which they can change instantly, creating hypnotic patterns. But don't get too mesmerized. Even though they have a funny name, flamboyant cuttlefish are predators that use a modified tongue to spear small prey. Unlike many other types of cuttlefish, squid, and octopus, flambos walk around on their tentacles and rarely swim. In fact, when confronted by a predator, flamboyant cuttlefish usually just flash their beautiful colors rather than flee. This has led some scientists to believe they are warning potential predators that they are poisonous!

POM-POM CRAB

Pom-pom crabs likely wouldn't be too happy with you calling them that. These guys are small but tough, and they probably wouldn't fancy themselves as cheerleaders. They might prefer their other name: boxer crabs.

Although these crabs are tiny, about the size of an adult human's pinky nail, and they don't have strong shells like other crabs, they have a fascinating alternative way of protecting themselves. The "pom-poms" on each of their claws are actually tiny sea anemones (really small versions of the same animal that clownfish live in), which sting other fish. The crab collects anemones and then uses them to defend itself. How the anemones live on the crab is a mystery!

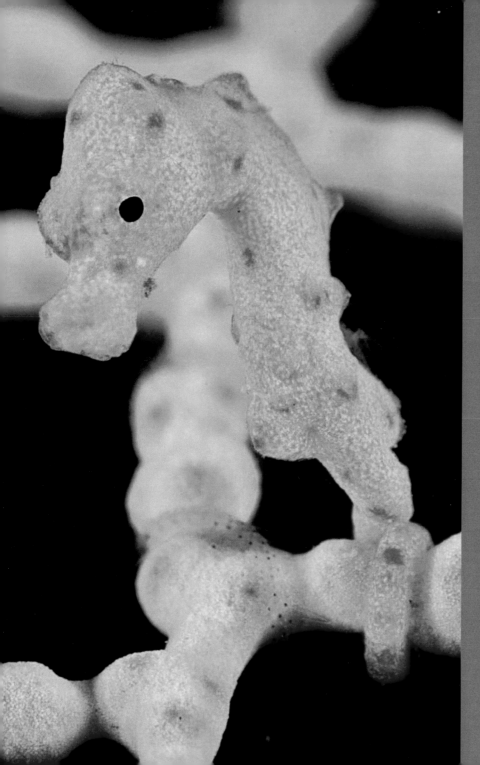

PYGMY SEAHORSE

A pygmy seahorse is definitely appropriately named! Most seahorses are the size of your hand or bigger, but this little guy is smaller . . . much smaller. The pygmy seahorse maxes out at three centimeters! That's about an inch. Most of them are the size of your pinky nail. How do these little guys protect themselves? Well, they look just like the coral they live on, making them almost impossible for other animals to find! Seahorses are unique in nature because the males give birth, and pygmy seahorses are extra-special because the males have pouches where they raise their young, as kangaroos do. The pygmy seahorse is small indeed but full of surprises!

FROGFISH

Frogfish aren't frogs at all! They are, in fact, some of the best hunters in the sea, and they barely move at all to catch their prey. These fish are all different sizes and have fantastic camouflage. One particular type of frogfish, a hairy frogfish, is so funny-looking most other fish don't even realize it's a fish! Amazingly, frogfish have a fishing rod on the top of their head. They wave this rod around to draw in little fish who want to see what's going on, and then— *wham*! The frogfish swallows the poor little fish in one gulp. That's similar to what an angler (a fisherman) does: uses a fishing pole and line to catch a fish. Maybe that's why they also have another name: the anglerfish!

HARLEQUIN SHRIMP

To humans, harlequins are masked clowns. But to sea stars, harlequin shrimp are no joking matter. This type of shrimp is secretive and beautiful, reaching no more than two inches long and sporting a white body with iridescent bright blue spots. What it's best known for, however, is its voracious appetite for sea stars (also commonly called starfish). Harlequin shrimp feed almost exclusively on sea stars, using their claws to flip them over so they can't run away. In fact, this shrimp is sort of a hero of the ocean because it's one of the few animals that's a predator to the crown-of-thorns sea star. The crown-of-thorns sea star has become a major threat to coral reefs as global warming has created an environment that has allowed them to grow in numbers and eat more coral than some reefs can sustain. Luckily, harlequin shrimp love to eat them. Another sea creature that's not clowning around!

STARGAZER

A stargazer under the ocean? How can it be? A stargazer gets its name because its eyes are on the top of its head, so it always appears as if it is staring up at the sky. Even more, many times its eyes are the only part of the fish that can be seen, as the rest of it is buried in the sand. A stargazer buries itself to stay hidden from its prey—small fish, shrimp, and crabs—with only its eyes slightly visible so it can seek out a bite to eat. Once it spots its prey, the stargazer opens its gigantic mouth and sucks in to create a vacuum, swallowing the prey whole. So, while the stargazer may look like it's just leisurely looking at the stars, it's actually focused on its next meal!

BOBBIT WORM

When we hear the word *worm*, we usually think about harmless slimy critters crawling around in dirt. But don't tell that to the bobbit worm, one of the ocean's most ruthless predators. The worm, which is about one inch in diameter but normally grows to about three feet long (although some have been recorded as long as 10 feet!) buries almost its entire body underground, with only its five antennae above the surface. Once the antennae sense prey, the bobbit worm shoots out of the ground and latches onto its meal with razor-sharp teeth. Sometimes it attacks with such speed that it can slice a fish in half! And if that doesn't work, the worm is equipped with toxin that it can inject into its prey to stun them. Now, that is not your average garden worm!

Jawfish have a confusing name—why are they named after their mouth? While many fish aren't famous for sharing strong family bonds, jawfish are some of the best daddies in the world. Male jawfish care for eggs in their mouth to make sure their babies are protected until they are old enough to swim. Other animals that want to eat jawfish babies won't mess with their big dads. Now that's using your jaw!

There are over 80 species of jawfish, which range in size from less than four inches to more than 18 inches. Some are beautiful, with yellow heads and blue bodies. Others are a drab gray. One thing they all have in common, though, is that they are great daddies.

JAWFISH FACTS

- SIZE: 4–18 inches
- HABITAT: Most tropical water
- DIET: Zooplankton
- FUN FACT: Most jawfish are around four inches, but the giant jawfish can be almost two feet long.

LEAF-NOSED EEL

No, this eel's nose is not a leaf, but it's pretty wild looking nonetheless. The beautiful eel, which can be yellow, blue, or black, depending on if it's a baby, male, or female, reaches up to 3.3 feet in length. However, only the very top of the eel is usually above the sand. The eel spends most of the day "sniffing" around in its hole, and that nose has some leaf-shaped protrusions that attract unsuspecting fish. When the fish are close enough, the eel gulps them up! These eels are rarely seen swimming freely, but when they are, they are beautiful, gliding around the ocean in an S-shape. That's why they are also called the ribbon eel.

BLUE-RINGED OCTOPUS

The blue-ringed octopus sounds harmless enough, but this small creature would be better named for its most startling trait: it's one of the most venomous animals in the world. The blue-ringed octopus maxes out at around eight inches and is bright yellow with, you guessed it, deep-blue-ringed spots. While it may look beautiful, the blue-ringed octopus is deadly. It catches its prey and then injects it with venomous saliva with a bite from its small beak. So if you see this octopus, think twice before getting too close to its blue spots!

MANTIS SHRIMP

Mantis shrimp aren't so shrimpy! While they usually reach only four inches long and weigh less than a cell phone, a mantis shrimp is no wimp. Pound for pound, it might be one of the toughest creatures in the ocean. It uses a modified arm to attack prey, and it does so with a deadly combination of speed and strength. It can punch with more power than a bullet and 50 times faster than the blink of an eye. That's similar to a human being able to break through a steel wall. You'll only laugh at a mantis shrimp once!

MANTIS SHRIMP FACTS

- SIZE: 4–15 inches
- HABITAT: Shallow reefs of the Indian and Pacific Oceans
- DIET: Mostly crustaceans
- FUN FACT: Mantis shrimp have the most sophisticated eyes of any animal.

GHOST PIPEFISH

With a name like ghost pipefish, you might think this a spooky animal. But actually, the ghost pipefish, a relative of the seahorse, is one of the most gentle, slow-moving fish in the ocean. Ghost pipefish are named because when they are babies, they're transparent like ghosts. As they grow older, however, they can take on many different types of colors and patterns, from yellowish-red to a Halloween-like black and orange, to completely green. Despite their elaborate colors and strange narrow body shape, they are able to camouflage quite well. Unlike with ghosts, divers love to encounter this pipefish!

SNAKE EEL

Is it a snake? Is it an eel? Despite the confusing name, snake eels are actually eels, but they look more like snakes than fish! In addition to having pointy heads and sharp teeth, many different types of snake eels are finless, giving them the slender appearance of a snake. This body type allows them to bury into the ground to avoid predators and help sneak up on prey. However, their snake-like appearance has another advantage: some species have coloring similar to sea snakes. Most predators know to stay away from sea snakes because they are venomous, and snake eels trick these predators into staying away as well. I guess the snake eel is confusing after all!

HAPPY CRITTERS, HAPPY CORAL, HAPPY EARTH

Almost all of the animals mentioned in this book make their homes in tropical coral reefs. The ones that don't live near the reefs and depend on them for food and nourishment. In fact, coral reefs support 25 percent of all marine life! They are tremendously important to the oceans. And the oceans are absolutely vital to humans, who rely on their inhabitants for food, such as the seafood you eat in restaurants; medicine, including treatments for HIV and cancer; and many other necessary parts of life.

Coral reefs are found all over the oceans, and they have survived for tens of thousands of years. However, they are now under a real threat from climate change and destructive fishing practices. Global warming has made the ocean too warm for many reefs, creating what's known as coral bleaching, when the reefs experience mass coral death and turn white. Additionally, some fisherman drag nets on the bottom of the ocean to catch shrimp and bottom-dwelling fish. This rips up the coral reef and can cause permanent damage. If coral reefs die, then all these amazing animals, including clownfish, won't be able to survive either.

Humans rely on coral reefs for so much, yet we are destroying them at alarming speeds. To help reefs, use resources like the Seafood Watch (www.seafoodwatch.org) to make sure you are eating sustainable fish. And support efforts to reduce your carbon footprint, including supporting policies to reduce global warming. If we don't take action now, we may lose coral reefs and all the life they support forever. Now, that's not funny either.

ABOUT THE AUTHOR

Matt Weiss is an award-winning photographer, journalist, dive expedition organizer, and filmmaker. He is also the author of *Please Be Nice to Sharks*. Matt's favorite shark is the biggest one of all, the whale shark, but he also loves all the small critters that live in the ocean. Matt has contributed to many international publications, including *Sport Diving Magazine*, *National Geographic*, and *Asian Geographic*. He is constantly searching for new ocean animals to photograph and spends lots of time on the bottom of the sea looking for small fish and crustaceans. His favorite place to dive is Antarctica, but when he's not swimming with sharks, he's the publisher of *DivePhotoGuide.com*, the world's largest underwater photography publication. Matt lives in Brooklyn, New York.

INDEX

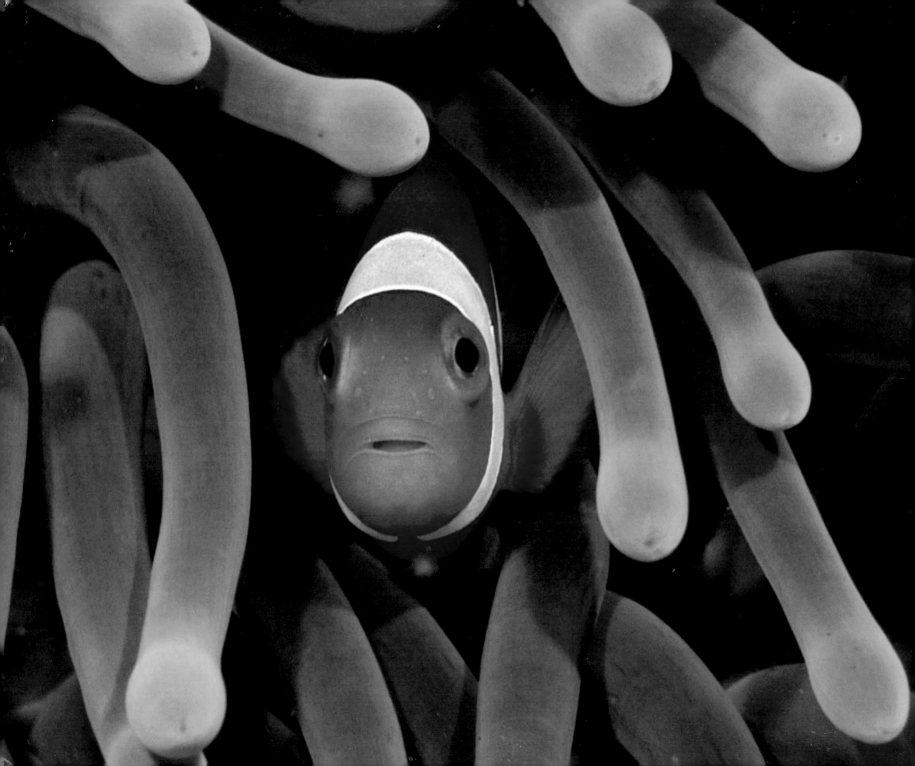